# It Was on My Mind

To Estelle Heard
My New Daughter (with love)

August Lastrappe

*[signature]*

(Page 46)

# It Was on My Mind

## August LaStrappe

**To order additional copies of this book, contact:**
Xlibris
1-888-795-4274
www.Xlibris.com
Orders@Xlibris.com
718426

# CONTENTS

## Chapter 8: Let Them Rest, if You Will

## Chapter 9: Agape' Love for Family & Friends

# INTRODUCTION

The things I write, what's on my mind,
The Holy Spirit talks and I give Him time.
The things I wrote was the way I feel,
At that particular time it was all for real.
My first poem was about he had nothing to do,
Kids in Joliet prison and they didn't have a clue.
Life should be about trying to do better,
I started out with Ruthie from the first day I met her.
I went to Africa and it was suppose to be a thrill,
But the poverty I saw, not in books it was all for real.
A couple of my poems came with a beat,
I rapped for R.L. Manaway and he couldn't stay in his seat.
I've written poems at funerals and really felt alone,
Love ones and friends, I looked around and they were gone.
Some are a joke just to see you smile,
To see people happy I'll walk a mile.
Other's about my youth and there's quite a few,
I'm sure you will agree that's my point of view.
All my writings some people say they're fine,
The things the Holy Spirit say; what's on my mind.

August "Bubber" LaStrappe

# DEDICATION

Who inspired me to live a Christian life; first my mother, Doris Hamilton (Mudear), my wife Ruthie Malone LaStrappe, and my friends:

Deacon Governor Green, his famous words were "Bubber I experienced that thing."

Rev. James Lamont Wallace—the scripture that stuck with me, Philippians 4:8.

Rev. Robert L Manaway Sr., his words were, "check it out; study God's word for yourself."

Rev. Gregory Bolden—When I was down and wanted revenge, Mark 11:26.

Deacon Beverly Richardson, and I never will forget, Lamentations 3:21-26.

Believing in my heart that God works with man, through man.

August "Bubber" LaStrappe

# THANK YOU

I would like to thank Doris LaStrappe, my daughter,
For typing my poems and putting them in order.

My wife Ruthie LaStrappe; after 46 years she's still by my side,
My love for her is so strong and that you cannot hide.

All my children; August P., Lisa L., Terry L., Doris L., and
August L. the third,
They say they like my poems; that includes every word.

Also, this has no rhythm or no rhyme,
Thanking Elder Avon Randle, and Dioncqua Cooper for
giving me some time.

And finally to Sam Blackwell for taking this cover picture,
Now when people reach for my book, they'll purchase it
quicker.

# CHAPTER 1

# TRIBUTE TO MUDEAR

# WHAT WE HAVE

What we have my sister and I,
A perfect mother and that's no lie.

She did a job on raising us,
Lots of love with very little fuss.

Our father died, I was yet a lad,
The love we got, others wished they had.

What we have is a mother that's sweet, and she's pretty too,
Nothing in the world for her, we wouldn't do.

Our mother is sweet, gentle and kind,
Mother's like that is hard to find.

What we have, my sister and I,
A mother so perfect, I could cry.

We didn't' get everything we wanted for that I cried,
Looking back now, Mudear, she really tried.

I don't remember our mother for us to be mad,
Our only regret, we missed our dad.

We have our own families, now that we are grown,
Her advice was to pray, and you must go on.

What we have my sister and I, and others would say the same,
Doris Hamilton is tops and should be in the hall of fame.

We love you Mudear, it's not hard to express,
We thank God for you, 'cause He gave us the best.

Our mother is a lady to love, and you don't have to try,
That's what we have, my sister and I.

What we have, Pauline and me,
Rita came later, and that made three.

Happy Mother's Day Doris Hamilton, and all year long,
May the rest of your life be filled with a song.

August (Bubber) LaStrappe

# MUDEAR'S SIDE

As we come together to spend a little time,
I'm writing this note—and I hope is rhymes.

For my family, and it's not that many,
We could have gone to a restaurant, or at least to Denny's.

Precious memories and we all have a lot,
I don't have them all, because some I've forgot.

I'm told the old people in Africa would sit around and tell the story,
Just like the Israelites, but they gave God the glory.

I have read the Bible and I use it as my guide,
Thanking God for you, on Mudear's side.

This is not about what you are doing or where you been,
It's all about family and 'cause we're kin.

If you follow the LaStrappe genes, we would have to take a ride,
But, today I'm concentrating on you, that's Mudear's side.

I'm so happy to see you, because it means so much,
You are my family, let's stay in touch.

We are crossing over one by one,
Fast approaching the setting sun.

I'm getting older and I can see clear,
We need to love each other, while we're here.

Before I close this note, and I won't read it twice,
Introducing Ruthie, she's my wife.

Meet my children and become a friend,
If for no other reason, 'cause we're kin.

I'm in love—I'm in love, listen I'm in love, and I'll spread it wide,
This is just for you on Mudear's side.

This poem is for you from the depths of my soul,
You are my family, that's what I've been told.

To all the girls, boys, ladies and that man,
We are related, so call me while you can!

August (Bubber) LaStrappe
06/29/2009

# CHAPTER 2

# MY LOVE, SWEETIE PIE, APPLE OF MY EYE

# Anniversary #10

It has not been easy, but I will make it up,
Living with me I know was a bitter cup.

It was not easy in the early years,
But you stayed right there, through all the tears.

I know I did wrong, but I've changed my ways,
I'll be loving you now the rest of my days.


I know I love you now, but I didn't know then,
The things I pulled will never happen again.

Your love is so strong that it made mine grow,
How you put up with me, God only knows.

Some men might have a wife that will pass the test,
I know now that God gave me the best.

Some men might brag and talk about their wife,
I know mine is the best part of my life.

Today is our 10th Anniversary, and I'll say it out loud,
With you by my side, makes me really proud.

To keep you buy my side, I'll follow any map,
Knowing I have your love, Ruthie LaStrappe.

Your Bubber
A.A. LaStrappe
10/26/1979

# HAPPY VALENTINE RUTHIE

## "The Word is Love"

The word is love, sometime hard to find,
When I met you! At last true love was mine.

Not like the sun and moon, that goes up and down,
Your love is straight and never turned around.

A tree points in one direction,
Like your love, never loses its affection.

The word is love and it has to be shown,
It starts from nothing and look how it's grown.

Like a baby that starts from birth,
My love for you is the biggest thing on earth.

Love from the third century was not the start,
My love for you is strictly from God.

Happy Valentine Ruthie, my darling wife,
When I married you, that started my life.

A.A. LaStrappe
(Your Bubber)

# Love That Last

It's about time you did something for your woman, your girlfriend, or your wife,
When it comes to mine, she's top shelf of my life.

You shouldn't have to wait for only one day of the season,
Giving honor to your wife for no particular reason.

Likewise ye husbands, dwell with your wife accordant to knowledge,
That doesn't take a degree, not even in college.

Nevertheless, let everyone of you love your wife as yourself,
Follow God's plan or you might get left.

If you take that woman to be your wife,
Love and honor her, the rest of your life.

Finding a wife is a good thing and you get favor from God,
Treat her like a queen, there is a reward.

Sometime Ruthie might call me and she could be becking,
You call me hen peck; she's the only hen pecking.

This is just for Ruthie—
Roses are red and violets are blue and that's a lot of fun,
After 46 years "Ruthie" you still number 1.

P.S., if any of you would like to use these lines,
Just remember to love your wife with a heart that binds.

This is the love month, February, and it's Valentine,
I thank God for Ruthie; are you still mine?

Forty-six years ago out of Chicago, and that's on the map,
Telling the whole world, I love you; I'm Bubber Strap.

August (Bubber) LaStrappe
02/2015

# Ruthie at 50 Years Old

If it had not been for the Lord who was on my side,
He would have not made Ruthie to be my bride.

If it had not been for the Lord who was on my side,
The reason we're still together, I let God be my guide.

When I first met you, you was 18 years old, and I was 26,
I had no idea what I was doing, but you see God was in the mix.

You have been my wife for 32 years,
Knowing you are by my side, there are no fears.

You were 18 then, and 50 is what you've made,
I want you to know my love for you will never ever fade.

You see your sisters and brother enjoying this event,
It had to have been God or at least heaven sent.

I want to end this poem, and I hope you know what I mean,
Listen to this song, and then I'll move off the scene.

To keep you by my side, I'll follow any map,
To know I'll have your love Ruthie LaStrappe

Your Bubber

# Ruthie!!! What Love

What is love that I might know,
How far does a man really have to go?

What love is this I hear,
Am I able to hold it close and near?

What is love; Can it be heard,
What is love, or is it just a word?

What love is this I hear,
Is it only found in someone dear?

What is love? What is love? Is it found in the rain, is it found in the trees,
That some love I'm led to believe.

What is love, does it have a color, is it read or is it blue,
What is love that can be held so true?

What is love, is it big, is it strong,
Is it something that can do no wrong?

What is love that I might know?
What is love that I might feel?
My love, your love, something for real!

For Ruthie LaStrappe
A.A. LaStrappe
(Your Bubber)

# That's Her

It's been a minute since I've talked about that girl,
Next to Jesus, she's the joy of my world.

You might talk about your wife in a negative tone,
If not for mine, I couldn't go on.

After all these years she's still smart, and pretty too,
my love for her grows and grows, just like new.

Ruthie, Ruthie, Ruthie Malone,
My love for you just keeps getting strong.

If you want to get married and need advice,
Simply put, you must follow Christ.

The years have passed and it's forty-three,
Me without Ruthie, I just can't see.

When you talk about a Christian marriage as though it were,
My wife is Ruthie LaStrappe, well, that's her!

(Your Bubber)
5-8-2012

# YOU ALREADY KNOW

After 41 years and we will go on,
My love for you is still growing strong.

Without you there is no me, and that's for sure,
God on our side, that makes it pure.

You gave me children and that part is done,
I forgot how we got them, but it was fun.

Life without you, I could never see,
We could make some more babies, at least maybe three.

This poem is for you, just for a smile,
I hope you wrap it up, and put it in your file.

If you don't think I love you, I'll call you on the phone,
And let the whole world know, it's Ruthie Malone.

p.s.
Oh, the thought about more babies was really great,
Then I realized my age, "Damn," I'm 68.

All my love, All my love, All my love
Your Bubber

# CHAPTER 3

## MY SPIRIT MIND

# Brain Washed

If you are not brain washed stand and raise your hand,
There is something about life you don't understand.

You have been given choices, and it's only two,
The one you pick, it's really up to you.

There is a God, a Spirit you have never seen,
Just open your heart if you're not too mean.

I don't have to follow God, but that's my choice,
In the still of the night, I do hear His voice.

Don't get me wrong, there is another voice to pick,
My experience tells me it's just another trick.

I wanted to rob a bank, and the feeling was really strong,
God's Spirit spoke; fool you know that's wrong.

There are two spirits that talk; you must follow one,
I'm brain washed with Jesus, that's God's only Son.

The other spirit will tell you, you can get away,
It will all come to a head, on that judgment day.

I am brain washed and I've made my choice,
I will follow God, and listen to His voice.

August (Bubber) LaStrappe
02/14/2012

# CHOICES

If you can read this letter, it's not too late,
Concentrate on Jesus, you don't have to wait.

You hail to Mary, but she's not the one,
Trust in Jesus, that's God's begotten Son.

Confessing to the pope won't save your soul,
Read your bible and the truth he will unfold.

There are lots of religions you can add or subtract,
In the end you will be judged and that's a fact.

Come unto me all you weary and heavy laden,
Look like the Mormons come straight from Satan.

Scientology is a cult that's spreading really wide,
You need to read your bible, let that be your guide.

What do Baha'is uphold and believe from the bible?
Accept the whole bible as it is, or you will be liable.

Suppose to be a holy Quran, that left Jesus far behind,
If you don't follow Jesus, you just lost your mind.

There is no such thing as a sun god, moon god; there is
only one,
That's Jehovah Elohim and His only begotten Son.

In the still of the night you can hear His voice,
The Holy Spirit will talk; again that's your choice.

August (Bubber) LaStrappe
07/14/2012

# CHURCH HOPPERS

I can't remember it all, so I thought I'd write it down,
The reason you leave the church and the excuses I have
found.

They beg too much and it's all about money,
Some of the reasons they give, is downright funny.

If he preach God's word, and it's simple and plain,
Why would you leave the church, because you're that vain.

Hopping from church to church must mean you are
confused,
Or do you go to church just to be amused.

You are going to another church, what will you add?
When they really get to know you, who will be sad?

Do you want to be a Christian and really stick?
Listening to God's word, it's not a simple trick.

No deposit, no return,
If you don't live for God, in hell is where you will burn.

August (Bubber) LaStrappe

# DON'T TALK

Don't talk about it if they didn't' do well,
Life is kind of strange, but there is always a story to tell.

Don't talk about it if they didn't achieve success,
That all depends on what it means, more or less.

If you graduated and have your piece of paper,
But, you look down on others; it's no more than mere vapor.

Don't talk if love you cannot show,
If not for the grace of God there you go.

We all made it, because we are still here,
Thank God for His blessings, that's what I hold dear.

Don't say nothing if I'm broke and really not that wealthy,
Success means I have joy, and I'm half way healthy.

Sometime we talk too much and don't know the real story,
Start thanking God and give Him the glory.

As we travel through life in our individual walk,
If you can't say something good, just don't talk.

As I realize that it's God who has kept us all,
If you trust in Jesus, you too can stand tall.

As I come to a close, and it's not over yet,
If you want success, Jesus you can get.

If you have done good and God has blessed you well,
Pray for others, now that you should tell.

If you don't like this poem, throw it down and walk,
But for the love of God, just don't talk.

August (Bubber) LaStrappe
03/28/07

# Forgot

Read the Old Testament, and travel back in time,
Give me a second and I'll try to make it rhyme.

As long as Moses' arms were held toward the sky,
God would win all battles; none of His people had to die.

God said you will be my people, and I will be your God,
If you follow my instruction, it won't be hard.

God will protect, and guard you staying under His wing,
The people were evil, and shouted give us a king.

I forgot how God led His people from slavery to the promise
land,
We need to turn back to Him and follow His plan.

I forgot about Sodom and Gomorrah, the city full of sin,
Homosexuality in that day, and we're doing it again.

We don't need a president or a king to tell us what is just,
Don't forget what's on our money! In God we Trust.

History will repeat itself, learn from that mistake,
Look to God to forgive you, that's all it take.

There should never be an abortion, but it's up to you to
decide,
Your sins are ever before you, and that you cannot hide.

Teach your children God's ways, if they want to hear it or not,
Never let them use my excuse and say!! I forgot.

August (Bubber) LaStrappe
2/20/12

# HANDLE WITH CARE

Handle with care means to be gentle, and take your time,
When it comes to God's people, you must be kind.

Dealing with God's people, and that's sinners too,
If you have any wisdom you know what to do.

Handle with care with humanity and grace,
God loves all mankind, that's the human race.

Be ye all of one mind having compassion for one another,
If there life is full of sin, they are still your brother.

With meekness, longsuffering forbearing one another in love,
You will be blessed by God, the promise that comes from
above.

Handle with care; you can be angry and sin not,
You are trying to get to heaven, because hell is really
too hot.

If my life is bad, and headed in the wrong direction,
Come to me with compassion using love and affections.

We're all God's people; our sins we must bear,
Pray for me daily, and remember, handle with care.

August (Bubber) LaStrappe
2/7/12

# Hitch Hiking on Easter

Driving down the highway of life,
I picked up a man, it's Jesus Christ.

He told me He had died a long time ago,
I had heard it, but I really didn't know.

I drove about five miles ahead,
He told me He could save me, that's what He said.

Now I didn't believe Him and I didn't know why,
I felt really strange, and I started to cry.

I asked him how far did He want to ride,
He said all the way til' heaven open wide.

He told me not to worry and have no fear,
Whenever I need Him, He's always near.

We drove up a mountain, that really got rough,
I know I couldn't make it, it was just too tough.

He held out His hand, and I put it in mine,
We climbed the mountain, in the nick of time.

He told me he had saved me from seen, and unseen danger,
I felt real bad; to me He was a stranger.

Now I know He died and rose to stay,
His Holy Spirit is with me all the way.

Traveling down the highway of life,
I cannot forget the day I met Christ.

He rose in my life, and he'll do it for you,
Just open your heart and let Him come through.

He's still here on the highway of life,
Why not let him in, it's Jesus Christ.

This is the day he rose from the dead,
Read your bible, and do what He said.

August (Bubber) LaStrappe
04/05/1980

# HOW TO PRAY

How to pray when you are wrong,
Ask God to please make you strong.

You are wrong and trying to get right,
A sincere prayer, with all your might.

God is able to see you through,
Why not trust Him, that's up to you.

You say you don't know, because God you have never seen,
Just believe in His word, and you can live clean.

You say dear God, I'm a wretch thoroughly undone,
I thought all life was just to have some fun.

Now I know there's a better way,
I'll trust in God and what He say.

Dear God, guide my mind and my feet,
Only your commandment is what I'll keep.

August (Bubber) LaStrappe

# INTERRACIAL???

Interracial marriage, do you really have a clue?
When God made Adam and Eve, He only made two.

God created Adam from the dust of the ground,
If my color is right, I think that's brown.

God made Adam and Eve and there was no sin,
You don't want mix marriages because the color of the skin.

There is no such thing as interracial marriage when a
woman marries a man,
You're looking at the color, but that wasn't God's plan.

You call it interracial when the skin tone is not the same,
The real dark and light skin get married, there should be no
shame.

God made the world and put it all together with perfect pieces,
If you give me a moment, I'll give an exegesis.

Interracial comes from the word inter (a prefix meaning) to
mingle with one another,
A man should be able to marry any woman, regardless to
the color.

You call it black, white, red, yellow, and even brown,
There is only one human race, and if you trust God you are
heaven bound.

Interracial; an adjective involving or representing different
race,
God made only one kind of humans and blessed us with His
grace.

It's not interracial it they both believe in Jehovah,
I hope you understand that, and this poem is over.

August (Bubber) LaStrappe
09-24-11

# It's in the Book

Lamatations 3:21-26, if you read that and stamp it in your mind,
I'll explain a few scriptures and try to make it rhyme.

It is only the Lord's mercies that we haven't been wiped out,
Study the history of the Bible; that should move your doubts.

God made the whole world and that was a master plan,
Everything was perfect and then he created man.

God said everything will be right when you hear my voice,
Then he told man I'm giving you the choice.

For God so loved the world that He gave us His only begotten Son,
That whosoever believes, the victory we will have won.

And if it seems evil unto you to serve the Lord and you're not too mean,
Read the Book of Joshua, chapter 24 and verse 15.

Remember the wisdom that is from above is first pure, if you would only take a look,
Where God's plan for man is found, it's in His Book.

How man should think, have a good life, and can make it great,
Read the Book of Philippians, chapter 4 and verse 8.

The earth is the Lord's and everything in it,
It's up to you to choose on how you will spend it.

All things work for the good and you might not understand,
Just trust in God's word; that's His master plan.

If we confess our sins, He is faithful and just to forgive,
That's the moment your life will change and then you begin to live.

Finally be ye all of one mind, having compassion for one another,
That's proof that you are saved, because you now love the brother.

Remember Deuteronomy 30:19; blessing and cursing therefore choose,
If you don't go with Jesus, Heaven you are bound to lose.

From Genesis to Revelations, you need to stop and take a look,
God's plan for man is right there; it's in the book.

August (Bubber) LaStrappe
8/29/11

# Just Like That

That's an adjective, indicated as different; do it this way, not
that way,
Right or wrong that's what God say.

You make plans for your life, and it seems to be set,
The future looks bright, things change just like that.

Time moves fast, and is really not that long,
Put your trust in Jesus, and never be wrong.

Leaving church, thinking of God's word, and a great singer,
Somebody makes you angry, and you give them the finger.

Just like that, Satan will pull your chain,
You lose if for a moment and it's all in vain.

Get up early in the morning making plans for your day,
Good and evil are before you remember what God say.

Situation changes and it looks like they went terribly wrong,
The valley and shadow of death really don't last that long.

Remember God got your back, and on that you can bet,
He will catch you before you fall, just like that.

When God's word is just in your head, that's information,
When God's word is in your heart, that's inspiration.

Trust God's word because that's where it's at,
Forget the preposition, and get to heaven, just like that.

Jesus will return faster than a twinkling of an eye,
You miss heaven and go to hell, and you wonder why.

It's no secret and you don't have to wonder what you
can get,
Romans 10:9 says you can be saved, just like that.

P.S.
Oh taste and see that the Lord is good,
If you haven't tried that, well maybe you should.

August (Bubber) LaStrappe
10/21/2011

# CHRISTIAN HANDS CHILDREN HOME 2003
## (MARTHA'S PLACE)

A ray of hope, a spark of light
At least thirty-five children will eat tonight

With help from you and surely God's grace
There's so much to do at Martha's place

They come from all over Kenya with a bowed down head
All they want is a chance or at least to be fed

On the streets of Thika she's reaching out her hand
Trying to save the children, as many as she can

Teaching them to pray and trust in God
Just for a piece of bread, it really must be hard

I saw the rich land of Africa-Oh what a beautiful place
But the sadness of the people as I saw in their face

I saw no hope, but I know there is
Trusting in God while fighting back the tears

I saw little kids sniffing glue because they had nothing to eat
The high made them forget; some didn't have shoes on their feet

There were beautiful animals grazing and roaming with such grace
But I couldn't forget the work being done at Martha's place

Oh how beautiful is Africa with such a rich land
If only we could get together and give Martha a better hand

The beauty I beheld at that mountaintop
I just gazed and gazed I could hardly stop

Mount Kilimanjaro so tall and spread so wide
A state like Texas could easily hide

I had waited so long and now I see
The beauty of God in an Acacia tree

I've seen beautiful trees with so much grace
But none like the Acacia, it takes first place

I saw the mountain, all the animals, and that single tree
The beauty I beheld and yet my heart wasn't free

We need to do more for that beautiful black space
At least those thirty-five children at Martha's place

The people I met and, we all look the same
They embraced me with love and even gave me a name

As long as I live, and wherever I rome
Kariuki is the name, till God calls me home

The tribe I met and it felt so right
I became a Kikuyu one warm summer night

August LaStrappe is my God given name
But since I've been to Africa I will never be the same

They need our help and now is the time
So stand up for Jesus and show some sign

We cannot save them all but at least a trace
So let's do what we can at Martha's place

August LaStrappe

# Success

A desire; it's a task or something you can fill,
You might call that success, or is it just a simple thrill.

Success is very simple, if you open your eyes,
If you have greed in your heart you'll never be wise.

What I think or what it looks like, might not be right,
All depends on who's looking, or are you willing to fight.

I found success when I married my wife,
After 42 years she's on top of this side of life.

Success is an everyday event,
You wake up each morning, and choose how it'll be spent.

Good success comes in moments if you resist temptation,
Put your trust in Jesus that moves doubt and all frustration.

Christians have a future, and sinners have a past,
Put your trust in Jesus, success for you will last.

You don't call it success when you're playing a game,
That's only an achievement for man's sports hall of fame.

Success and what it looks like from my point of view,
You have a decision to make and that's up to you.

Real success and where it can be found,
Study God's word, its indubitable sound.

The secret of success, you must be wise,
Pray to God in heaven He'll open your eyes.

August (Bubber) LaStrappe
01/27/2011

# THE CLOSE OF ANOTHER YEAR

As we come to the end of another year,
You make a resolution, it starts right here.

The last few years you started out right,
Old Satan go busy, you lost the fight.

A new year and you start out strong,
Praying to God to do no wrong.

As we come to the end of another year,
You do have a job, the Bible is clear.

He that hunger and thirst, is a beautiful phrase,
Why not pray to God and consider your ways.

Paul says resist the devil and he will flee,
Stay close to God, the blessing you'll see.

As we come to the end of another year,
Here's a few things that I hold dear.

I will love all brothers and sisters too,
My number one plan, what about you?

I will pay my tithes and have no fear,
That's my resolution for the oncoming year.

I will do what's needed and lie to no man,
Another resolution, do the best I can.

My main resolution is to live for Jesus while I'm here,
As we come to the beginning of another year.

August (Bubber) LaStrappe

# The So Called Saint

Walking in, but not off the light,
No intentions of doing what's right.

The so called saint is easy to find,
Go to any church, you will see the sign.

Loves to shout to get attention,
All they want is to hear their name mentioned.

They will testify and make you cry,
A true saint will detect, it's only a lie.

They might pray a beautiful prayer,
See them tomorrow, they are drunk somewhere.

Looking and waiting for a mistake,
The gossip was started, that's all it takes.

They are able to sing and the Spirit is hot,
See them on Tuesday and they are smoking pot.

They are found all over the world in every race,
Throughout the globe in every place.

They know everybody's business, and lie without faint,
That's part of the life of a so called saint.

A.A. (Bubber) LaStrappe
1977

# TIME

It's time to stop acting and living wrong,
Ask God for help, He will make you strong.

It's time for you to learn not to hate,
That same God will guide you straight.

Do you know the time?
Look at the world, that's a definite sign.

It's time to stop, listen and look,
I turned to Jesus, that's all it took.

Man have tried all methods in every way,
Turn to God and hear what he has to say.

What time is it, don't you know?
Time to look to heaven, the best way to go.

You still have a chance; it's not too late,
A sincere prayer will set you straight.

God is calling all mankind,
Talk to Him, He's easy to find.

Do you have time to love or time to hate?
Your clock is running out, don't wait too late.

A.A. LaStrappe
(Bubber) 1976

# WANTED

Come unto to me, all ye that labor and are heavy laden,
The promises of Jesus that will keep you from Satan.

But the wisdom that is from above is first pure, and will
keep you clean,
You are wanted by God, that's James 3:17.

Wash me thoroughly from mine iniquity and cleanse me
from my sin,
No experience necessary for God is truly our best friend.

Being wanted by God, and on that we can boast,
When you've done all to stand listen to the Holy Ghost.

Wanted while you are yet alive, dead is too late,
Turn yourself in to Jesus, and you'll reach heaven's gate.

Behold I stand at the door and knock, Revelation 20,
Cast all your burdens on the Lord and don't withhold any.

You must believe; life is too short, hell is too hot, and
eternity is too long,
When you get to heaven's gates and find out that you were
wrong.

There is a bounty for your soul, and the price has been paid,
Jesus went to the cross, now we have it made.

Wanted, wanted, the choice is up to you,
Turn your life over to Jesus and He'll see you through.

II Corinthians 2:11; lest Satan should get the advantage of us,
Put all your trust in Jesus, and that you must.

Except God's wanted poster, and you'll be just fine,
The proof is in the Bible—Romans 10:9.

August (Bubber) LaStrappe
10/12/11

# Your Decision

How to get to heaven and it's in the book,
Deuteronomy 30:19, you need to stop and take a look.

It's set before you good and evil; choose if you're not too mean,
The Lord is forever near and always on the scene.

It's not hard to become a Christian with a made up mind,
Read the book of Romans, start at 10:9.

There's only two sides of life; good or evil, right or wrong,
You need to make a decision; don't wait too long.

God is patiently waiting and quick to forgive,
A sincere prayer; now you become to live.

Judgment day is coming and that's a fact,
When you see Jesus, will He turn His back?

New Destiny is a place where God's word runs totally free,
and it's plain to see where you need to be, and there is no fee, Bishop Ogletree.

August LaStrappe
11/18/2013

# YOUR MANIFESTATION

The manifestation of the promise of God will be seen,
No later than 2015.

Since I don't have but a minute and I'll do my best,
To explain the meaning of the word manifest.

Easy to see and you must understand,
Here at New Destiny there is a God sent man.

Come let us reason together and we all can see,
When it comes to knowing God's word, well, that's Ogletree.

Manifestation = a display, show or demonstration,
Time, talent and tithes are your reasonable expectation.

It's not all about money, but it's a part, you should take a look,
Don't take my word, why? It's in the book.

To experience manifestation you must come to a new place
of beginning,
How to start that? First you must stop sinning.

My help comes from the Lord who made heaven and earth,
How bad to you want your manifestation, that's what it's worth.

To experience manifestation you must have a one on one
encounter, Luke 9:62,
This room of Elders and Deacons, and you know that to do.

God works with man, through man in his own time,
Wait on the Lord, again wait, and heaven will be mine.

To experience manifestation you must endure until the end,
Trust in God and your manifestation will begin.

May you experience a year of blessing and manifestation,
If it don't come when you think, well, just be patient.

*Inspired by Estelle Heard and Bobby Miller*
August (Bubber) LaStrappe
2015

# CHAPTER 4

## MR. PRESIDENT! MR. PRESIDENT! OUR 1ST BLACK PRESIDENT

# I Wonder Why!

You say you are a Christian, and you believe in God,
To love all mankind, it shouldn't be that hard.

I wonder why I could feed your baby, and work in your field,
If I had an idea, that's what you would steal.

You told me I was a slave, and you I would always need,
I was fooled for a while, and then I learned to read.

I'm told if you wanted to hide anything from a black man just
write it down,
You need to study your black history, where the truth can
be found.

Your King James translated from Hebrew and Greek,
God's word in whatever language is what we need to seek.

I wonder why we knew about God before we crossed the big
ocean,
The Ethiopians got the word in Africa that started the
motion.

We could go to the armed forces, and fight for our nation,
Coming back home; sitting in the back of the bus station.

Some Europeans can dance and you claim Elvis was the king,
If he hadn't studied under black folks he couldn't do a thing.

I wonder why I didn't hear about the invention of the stop light until I was grown,
It wasn't in your history books, and you know that was wrong.

From 1789 to 1929 all your presidents owned slaves, and for that I could cry,
We finally got a black leader, and you hate his guts; I wonder why?

August (Bubber) LaStrappe
2/16/2012

# It's No Surprise

If you go to any prison, you'll find mostly black,
Some are doing life, just for selling crack.

Most went to court using a public defender,
The white man's law; mostly only a pretender.

If you spank your child you will go to jail,
They took prayer out of the school, that's where we failed.

All black men are bad and there is no hope,
Don't forget that white catholic priest; that includes the pope.

Taking advantage of little boys looks like a growing rate,
How about those allegations at Penn State?

You say all blacks are bad and that's just not right,
The two statements I just made, well, they are white.

It's no surprise if a black man steals a car and goes to the
Penn,
A white man gets psychological help and starts over again.

Seven cops beat and kick a black kid on the ground,
The media said you don't understand, because you don't
hear the sound.

Black people have been mistreated so long and it's no
surprise,
I'll use Maya Angelou's words, "Still we rise."

August (Bubber) LaStrappe
06-11-2012

# JUST THINKING

There was never a slave owner in America with a name like
Obama,
It's good he got his name from his father and didn't inherit it
from his mama.

The Europeans took our land and we forgot our name,
Raped our woman and beat us down, then considered us tame.

Most African Americans have used a slave name if you
check the history,
Where we really come from, it's nobody's mystery.

What would be wrong if I changed my name to Malcolm X,
You probably would amend you laws, so what's next.

A few common names we carry is either French, Dutch, and
surely European,
They made us forget our culture; being just that mean.

Barack Obama is not your average American name,
The only American president to prove his birth, it's a damn
shame.

When will black history become American history, and if it
ever will,
A few names in black history you never heard; that's for real.

Inventors in the 1800; Norbert Rillieux, Lewis Howard
Latimer, Jan Matzeliger,
Granville T. Woods; some you need to explore,
Check the real history, you will find many more.

New history, you'll find Rosa Parks and the statement she made,
Ida B. Wells Barnett did the same thing years earlier, don't let that fade.

New history, you'll find Babe Ruth and maybe Jackie Robinson, you claim open the door,
Charles Follis, first black professional football player in 1904.

Just thinking why a state like Florida could cast a vote,
And, 51 delegates changed it; it's the laws they wrote.

No president in history has ever been so closely scrutinized with every move he makes,
You should be watching that priest, and how many boys he rapes.

The morals in America are getting lower and lower, and really sinking,
Pen in hand, mind wondering and just thinking.

August (Bubber) LaStrappe
03-12-2012

# PAY ATTENTION

If you look at the White House from all the way back,
If you hadn't noticed, our president is black.

He gave us a lot of promise before he was elected,
Everything he tried, the senate has rejected.

Everywhere he goes he's trying to do right,
It looks like you're against him because he isn't white.

God will bless all mankind according to His book,
Prejudice is alive and well; just stop and take a look.

It's really sad you can't get over the color of my skin,
From all the way back, you classified that was a sin.

The Bible described Jesus' hair like lamb wool and feet like gold,
You drew blond, blue eyes in the pictures and books you sold.

It has been said that the black man was just dumb and really
strong,
But the way you describe Jesus, somebody was really wrong.

If we could only forget the color and look at the man,
None of us are perfect, but we're in God's hand.

If you read your Bible and study it right,
You'll discover the people, they all weren't white.

God loves all mankind, if only we could get along,
The rainbow of colors, that should make us strong.

No man is better than the other if you are paying attention,
The color of your skin, that's something that shouldn't be
mentioned.

Pay attention and you still can get it right,
If you make it to heaven, nobody is going to be white.

You claim Christianity; you should take a stand,
Follow the words of Jesus, and not the Klu Klux Klan.

The wisdom from above is first pure, that's James 3:17,
If you study the Bible and practice, you wouldn't be so mean.

We should pray for our president, not for the color of his skin,
Consider what's right, not who, and we all win.

This is the end of this little poem and that's a wrap,
Thanks for reading! I'm A.A. Strap.

August (Bubber) LaStrappe
8/24/11

# STILL OVERCOMING
# 12/07/08

When you read the book, and it's all said and done,
You will discover this, nothing new under the sun.

You have seen the past, that's what we call history,
The future looks bright; it's really not a mystery.

If you read the Bible, and it's in the book,
They marched around the walls; that's all it took.

Gideon's army; and you should know the story,
It's not what they did, they gave God the glory.

Non violence, and we were able to stand,
Think for a moment, that was God's plan.

Our families were split up, knowing not the direction,
Don't forget the lynching, plus that gonorrhea infection.

It was a long time coming, through slavery and degradation,
Over four hundred years of bad segregation.

Moving on up, and we must be kind,
Remember God's word, vengeance is mine.

When Obama gets to Washington, on Pennsylvania Street,
God will be with him, as he takes his seat.

Barak's name is in the Bible, if you really need a clue,
Read Hebrews Chapter 11, verse 32.

Obama is not the Savior, but he's playing a part,
Just follow God's spirit, it's not that hard.

A black man as President, and I hope you don't hate,
Concentrate on God, before it's too late.

President Obama, congratulations on having won,
All minorities should note it can be done.

                    August "Bubber" LaStrappe


P.S. if you are still looking for Barak and you need a little more,
Read the book of Judges, try Chapter four.

# THE CHANGE

Looking back and I remember when,
Things I couldn't do for the color of my skin.

This is for young blacks in case you didn't know,
The things from my experience should help you grow.

White and colored water, something you've never seen,
Back in my day, the white man was just that mean.

In the 40's, that's when I started school,
White was right, but we changed the rules.

We could go to the picture show, if you knew your place,
The rules were, never look a white man straight in the face.

In the 50's things was changing and I was here,
Going to Play Land Park; only once a year.

I saw it happened, I saw the change,
Only a young teenager, a new and wider range.

Colored, the back of the bus and you saw the mark,
Thank God for that day with Rosa Park.

I saw it happened I saw the move,
Black men marching, something he had to prove.

I like what happened, I loved that scene,
Black men moving, though I was in my teens.

We are moving on up, but not there yet,
Trust in God, for the future you will get.

There have been a lot of changes, since the year of '42,
Now that I'm older, it's kinda up to you.

We have grown greatly, with the color of our skin,
Thank God!!!! A black president in 2010.

With God on our side we can control the nation,
Before you do anything, you must get an education.

We are not a dumb people, and never been,
They tried to keep us down, for the color of our skin.

God has blessed us and we've come a long way,
Remember the words of Jesus, and pray every day.

August (Bubber) LaStrappe
01/03/2010

# CHAPTER 5

# LIFE IN CONROE

# And God Said!
# That's Good

In February of '42' I arrived on the scene,
You might remember my Mother, she ran the Teenage Canteen

God knew what he was doing, and it seemed so right,
The year I moved to Conroe, one warm summer night.
And God said! That's Good

Now here's where you will start,
The friends you will meet will remain close to your heart.

Time has passed and it's been so long,
The good memories I have just lingers on.

How special is the Reunion that we can meet again,
Just to meet and greet, while we still can.
And God said! That's Good

That, I remember so well;
All those good times, and lots of stories to tell.

To name a few of my classmates, while I still have the time,
Saying hi to Ben and Delores, you are always on my mind.

Bobbi Rose was sweet and such a lady indeed,
All the young ladies should stop and really take heed.
And God said! That's Good

Now don't start groaning, just remember when we were kids,
Oh, and say hi Frank Manning,

George Henderson, Roy Collins, and G. L. Lee,
At this reunion that's a few more that I would love to see,

Johnnie Mae, Ella, Laverne, and Bettie Sue,
Oh, hi Freddie, I got your card and the pictures too.
And God said! That's Good.

And I probably won't name them all,
But the remembrance of my classmates still stands tall.

Way back when I was yet a lad,
The good times as a kid that we often had.

I have not seen C. D., Juanita, or Roger since that
glorious day,
Marching down the aisle, and we went our separate ways.

I know I will see Stella; I always do,
Whenever I'm in Conroe or just driving through.
And God said! That's Good.

The memories I have, and I'm almost through,
You are always in my heart! THE CLASS OF '62'

I hope to see Big Laryon Carrie, I. J. Brown, and his sister as
well,
John Flewellen, Betty, Audrey, I'm sure we all have stories to
tell.

The last two friends I yet can claim,
Give me a second and I'll tell you their names.

Leodia Jones—the time I really cried,
He stole and wrecked his dad's car and almost died.

There was a time we were called Flap, and Bubber,
Between our friendships there was no other.

His name is James, Flap, Major Fleet, Flewellen,
Our friendship has lasted without any yelling.
And God said! That's Good

But what about you,
I have really been blessed since '62'

I didn't go to college like the rest of you,
I worked extra hard, something I had to do.

Whatever job I was on, I have never been fired,
I look back and smile, now that I'm retired.

Two daughters and three sons, the joy of my life,
There is only one better, I must include my wife.

Ruthie and I were married in '68'
My life changed, that's when I started straight.

Praying to God to do the things I should,
He looked down, and God said! Bubber that's good.

August A. LaStrappe Jr.
"Bubber"
3/7/03

# BACK IN THE DAY

As we grow older and I remember when,
We were young and pure, with very little sin.

Back in the day my school was across the street,
But at 12'o clock, the canteen is where we would meet.

We didn't have much and there was no greed,
If anyone was hungry, a hamburger Mudear would feed.

The black owned business, and there were quite a few,
We danced at the Canteen and Evan's, but not R-Q.

Back in the day there might be a fight and get a suspension,
There were no killings, or a murder, that wasn't the intention.

There was no gangs between pals Dugans and Melee quarters,
We all went to the same school and that was the order.

Growing up in Texas, and Conroe is the town,
During segregation and on that we'd frown.

It seem like black's were together with very little fuss,
Don't forget that colored water, plus the back of the bus.

As we grow older we should see it clear,
If not for the Love of God, we wouldn't be here.

Back in the day when we were young and pure,
God kept us all, and that's for sure.

We grew up and we all went different ways,
Holding fast the memories of back in the days.

August (Bubber) LaStrappe<br>07/26/2009

# Class of '62

Just thinking about my class mates,
My glasses became a little hazy

I just wanted to make you smile and say,
That Bubber is still crazy

It's been such a long time since we all been together,
To get everybody here was my greatest endeavor

As I look at you after 50 years,
I won't be long, so lend me your ears

Monday, May 28, 1962, at 8 PM,
26 kids marched down the aisle as they sang a hymn

We left that night headed in a different direction,
My love for you has never lost its affection

I lived in California-Chicago-Seattle and now I'm back home,
Remembering who I grew up with, I've never felt alone

Out of 26 graduates—8 of us has passed on,
We stop for a moment and bow our heads and maybe sing a
song

Erma Jean—IJ—Brenda—GL—Ella Lavern—Roger—Herbert
Lee—and Freddy,
That's a sure sign, at our age we need to get ready

You can trust Jesus, His word never fail,
If you make the wrong choice, you will go to hell

I hope you have made the choice on where you will end,
If you have Jesus in your heart you ought to tell your kin

Now that we are much older and I hope wiser too,
I'm here to say I love you and now I'm through.

August Bubber LaStrappe
5-30-2012

# I See Dead People

Driving around Conroe my old hometown,
I see dead people slowly walking around.

I talked to a few people, and I asked them twice,
The problem is, they just don't know Christ.

I see dead people, but it is not the end,
Just look to Jesus to forgive your sin.

I have Jesus, and I don't have to worry,
Thanks to my mother, Deacon Sadler, and the Rev. Curry.

They told me that Jesus is the only way,
Just follow his example, and pray every day.

Driving around Conroe and I remember back when,
When we were young and pure and there was no sin.

I see dead people and they shouldn't die twice,
Turn your life over and give it to Christ.

If you don't know how, it's not that hard,
Find a good preacher that talks about God.

I see dead people, I see dead people, but it's not over yet,
Give your life to Jesus and Heaven you can get.

August (Bubber) LaStrappe
11/04/07

# JUST A THOUGHT

I saw so many friends and some I had forgot,
Looked into your faces; that really meant a lot.

It made me think how GOD has blessed us all,
Life's ups and downs and we are still standing tall.

I know GOD has blessed you I saw it in your face,
I hope you realize, that's part of GOD'S grace.

We are moving on and the older get,
I hope you love Jesus, He's your only bet.

I love to have fun, and clown around too,
But serving Jesus Christ, that's all I want to do

I'm trying to end this poem and not make it too long,
Keep GOD on your side, and we all can stay strong.

God blessed the reunion and I hope to see you soon,
Next time I'll bring Ruthie and Pauline, I'll remind them
around June.
I'll see you in New Year's in 2005,
If GOD says· the same and we are still alive.

August LaStrappe
(Bubber)

# Booker T. Washington
# (Conroe)

If I could write a poem it would sound like this,
Going to school in Conroe would top the list.

Precious memories and we all have a few,
What I'm going to say, that's my point of view.

We all have memories, some good, some bad,
The friends that's gone before us, that makes me sad.

As I look around and this is what I want to say,
We are getting older, just look at my hair it's solid gray.

I do realize that it was God and God alone,
The one that I will trust until He calls me home.

I follow Jesus with all my heart and with all my soul,
When it's time for me to go, that's what I'll hold.

I'm not preaching, but I know and I know it well,
If you don't follow Jesus, you're going to hell.

This is another reunion and there has been quite a few,
Don't forget what I said, it's my point of view.

To all my classmates and friends hear what I say,
When you go to bed at night, don't forget to pray.

In two years from now your face I'll love to see,
Don't forget who we are, we're Booker T.

August (Bubber) LaStrappe
6-11-2015

# CHAPTER 6

# THINGS I WAS TOLD

# He Had Nothing to Do

*(revised from 1974)*

The land was dry, the sun was hot,
All he did was drink wine and smoke pot.

He lived in the city where there's lots of slums,
Gang banging was tops, so he ate bread crumbs.

He had no money to go to school,
Robbing his brother, that was rule.

He had nothing to do, but rob and steal,
It's not his fault, it was just a thrill.

The ghetto was blocked and he couldn't go further,
No father figure, not even a brother.

Black on black crime was everywhere,
White man was law, and they didn't care.

He had nothing to do, from birth to teens,
Now he's in jail, a life with no means.

A second chance at age 28,
There is no job that makes license plates.

Back in jail, and his life is through,
It all started, because he had nothing to do.

A.A. Lastrappe
(Bubber)

# MY TEACHERS

My youth up, I was told by grandmother (Pauline Hamilton)
and Doris (Mudear),
Always keep God in your heart, He's forever near.

Teaching me about God and how not to be afraid,
At an early age, it was only in my head.

When it's only in your head, you might not be sure,
But the wisdom from above is absolutely pure.

James Lamont Wallace, in Chicago Illinois,
Taught me about God, then I heard His voice.

We would sing all day, and then he would preach,
The Bible classes were great; boy that Lamont could teach.

His teaching got me interested in what God had to say,
Then I moved to Seattle, and met Robert Manaway.

R.L. Manaway preached God's word without any doubt,
The words hit my heart, so I had to shout.

Twenty-one years, I heard him preach and teach God's way,
Now I'm in Texas, and Ethan Ogletree, his sermons gets
an A.

My gradmother and Mudear gave me a start,
Listening to Rev. Wallace, put it in my heart.

R.L. Manway taught me really how to run,
Trusting in Jesus, God's only son.

Ethan Ogletree preaches and teaches like it's his last day on earth,
I'm on my way to heaven, and that's what it's worth.

Thanks to my grandmother, Mudear, Wallace, Manaway, and Ogletree, for pointing the way,
From Genesis to Revelation, read your bible and trust what God say.

August (Bubber) LaStrappe

# PASSING THROUGH

From 1960 to 2010,
In and out of jail, and going to the Penn.

Right after slavery they lost control,
They brought drugs to the ghetto, that's what we sold.

We couldn't get a job; they said we couldn't learn,
Remember the LA riot and how it really burned.

Trying to get your attention, you could plainly see,
All we wanted was a job, and that was key.

Still struggling in this, United State,
Black on black crime, that's a growing rate.

Drug dealing, gang banging and prostitution,
Somewhere in the middle there has to be a solution.

Not meaning to be critical, but I'm concentrating on blacks,
Don't blame the white man, because you still selling crack.

You can do better if you had a clue,
Get an education, that's really up to you.

Killing each other to protect a certain zone,
Fighting over property, you don't even own.

Sagging pants and you don't know the history,
It started in prison, and that's not a mystery.

Pull up your pants and walk like a man,
Praying to God, and do what you can.

In your reaching the moon, could be your goal,
Put God in your life, that'll save your soul.

August (Bubber) LaStrappe
01/08/2010
Inspired by Marget Chappel

# THINGS I WAS TOLD

Starting with eany, meany, miney, mo,
If you are of age, remember how it used to go.

I was told my hair was nappy, and mostly a disgrace,
Back in the day you couldn't look a white man in the face.

The Europeans have hid in the books they call history,
My cousin Steve's book (Who is Sambo) part of a mystery.

I was told my skin is dark and my lips are thick, Another put
down from a Caucasian's trick.

Study your history to see what they tried to hide, Lynching
and murder, but God is still on our side.

I was told we could only pick cotton, and work in the field,
Everything we had, the European was determined he had to
steal.

Raping Africans, and killing the Indian nation,
All for what they call progress, and their civilization.

In Heaven, separation between black & white with a different
roll,
I know that's a lie, but that's what I was told.

We could never be equal in this United States,
Nothing but lies, and deceit, and we fell for the bait.

Lynch gave a plan that kept us scared, and full of fear,
Now that we know that game, we can come up from the rear.

All the crooked lies, and games that they sold,
I was dumb enough to believe the things I was told.

August (Bubber) LaStrappe
2012

# CHAPTER 7

# WORDS TO THE SHEPHERD

Tabernacle M.B. Church
Seattle, WA
9/17/2013

# FOCUS ON THE RAP

*(Somebody hold my walking stick)*
This is my church, this is my church, and you called my name,
I'm a whole lot older, but I'm still the same.

I don't do rap, it's a lot of fun,
Forgot about my age, I'm 71.

I had to really focus and focus on your theme,
I'm still praising God if you know what I mean.

I stopped by to visit, to tell you what I know,
If you trust in God, it's the only way to go.

Your theme is on Focus, and focus on God,
Study God's word, it's not that hard.

Hocus Pocus Do-mo-no-mi-nokos,
If you hear a good sermon, you really got to focus.

This is my church, this is my church, and I'm right back home,
I'm here for just a minute, and I'll be gone.

You got a good preacher, that's all I got to say,
I can't spell his name but it's Manaway.

I'm on my way to heaven 'cause I got a good start,
It took a lot longer 'cause I'm not that smart.

I saw the word focus means to concentrate,
Follow God's plan and don't be late.

You got a good Pastor and he preach real good,
You trying to go to heaven, like you know you should.

I wrote this all down really, really quick,
Now that I'm through, give me my stick.

                              August (Bubber) LaStrappe

# Ingredients to Grow

Do you really want to grow and get close to God?
Pastor Ogletree is telling you it's not that hard.

A made up mind and study God's word,
The things he's telling you, you already heard.

You know right from wrong, and that's your choice,
Listen to Ogletree's words, it's in his voice.

Pastor Ogletree, a man of God, and he watches for your soul,
If you follow the instructions, you'll never grow old.

To be a Christian, you won't be sad,
At the end of your journey, we'll all be glad.

The moral of this is to straighten up and fly right,
When we get to heaven, we will be out of sight.

If you are a Christian, you should stand tall,
Priority is Jesus, and that's about all.

                                    August (Bubber) LaStrappe
                                    4/6/2011

# JUST BLESSED

Bishop Ogletree was teaching how to live a blessed life, all
through November,
If you are over 65 with a little wisdom you should remember.

God has said, choose this day whom you will serve,
He has blessed us all, this time with things we don't
deserve.

We should know by now; come unto me, I'll give rest,
All the temptations of life, and some we pass the test.

Living a blessed life should be plain to see,
Read Lamentations 21, that's in chapter three.

I don't think we are old, but we are getting there fast,
Put all your trust in Jesus something we know will last.

Through the years we keep on toiling, through the storm
and through the rain,
The ups and downs of life, trusting God and heaven we'll
gain.

Jesus is tenderly calling and we don't know the time,
Living the blessed life; trusting only the true vine.

God had placed us here to be a blessing, and that's in the
book,
James 5:20 you should stop and take a look.

If you want all God's blessing so life will be great,
Read Philippians chapter four, that's verse eight.

How to live a blessed life, pray every day and always remember,
Every time you wake up put Jesus on your agenda.

This is for the Patmos Ministry, of which I'm a part,
Telling others how to be blessed shouldn't be that hard.

August LaStrappe
12/11/2013

# MANAWAY RAP

The type of this poem I got to call it a rap,
It's my first time doing it, I'm double 'A Strap.

If the drummer don't mind got to give me a beat,
I tell you what I mean and try to make it sweet.

Now, I can rap and I know I can,
Robert L. Manaway is a God sent man.

He comes from the country buy the cotton field,
Preaching God's word and you know he's for real.

He got a lot of wisdom although he's kinda young,
You got to remember where it all comes from.

His name is Manaway, I said Manaway, that's Robert L,
Robert L Manaway.

Now he can play the organ and sing a song,
Between him and God he's never left alone.

I had a problem just the other day,
I called my pastor, he told me what to say.

He said pray Strap pray, pray Strap pray,
Don't stop to play, just pray, pray, pray.

I hope you listening 'cause I got something to say,
I love my preacher in a great big way.

I know God called him 'cause he preach to good,
You better start to listen like you know you should.

I'll spell his name so you can get it right,
When he preach God's word it's out of sight.

*M* is for Manaway that's his name, ask me again I'll tell you the same.
*A* is for All Mighty God, when he preach God's word he really preach it hard.
*N* is a letter I didn't know what to say, remember what he told me, God will make away.
*A* is alert that's he he is, it all comes from God so give Him some cheers.
Now *W* is next if I'm spelling it right, bother my preacher we might as well fight.
Moving right along and I'm not quite through, there's another *A*, I'll tell you what to do.
Now follow God's plan and stay real close, He'll make it plain through the Holy Ghost.
Coming to the end I see the letter *Y*, I love my preacher and that's no lie.
Put it all together and now I'm through,
If you want to go to heaven, he'll tell you what to do.

Dedicated to Pastor Robert L Manaway, Sr.
*Second pastoral anniversary*
*Originally written 10/08/1985*
A.A. LaStrappe

# PASTOR MANAWAY—
# 25 YEARS

I wanted to write a poem, and I hope you don't forget,
Turning back the time, and remembering the day we met.

Larry Dunson told me "there was a man that could change
your world,"
Everything was fine, except for that greasy Jerry Curl.

Twenty-two years of preaching, and I hardly missed a one,
You still talking about God and His only begotten son.

For a moment, let's visit the past and then I'll be through,
Go back to the first anniversary, but I started at number two.

That's when I did a rap, and I did it with humility and grace,
For those of you that were not here, I'll give you a little taste.

A new beginning and we are all excited about Obama,
But I want to tell you about Manaway, and what he learned
from his mama.

She taught him to have love and respect for all mankind,
It rubbed off on me, but that took a little time.

Give me a moment and I'll explain my situation,
When Obama gets into the White House, Manaway should
get an invitation.

Twenty-five years and your schedule is 24-7,
Telling people about God, and how to get to heaven.

Moses, Dr. King and the Patriots that stood very tall,
Manaway, just like Nehemiah, you must stay on the wall.

A new beginning and I'm told that's your theme,
Tab, you can follow Manaway, for God too has given him a
dream.

August (Bubber) LaStrappe
11/21/08

# REMEMBER

## *You didn't hear this from me*

I have some gossip I want to tell,
I went to the pastor's house and went through his mail.

There was one letter I'm not ashamed to say,
He prays and watch for your soul each and every day.

I peeped in his room and he was on his knees,
He was praying to God, he even said please.

I stayed over a long time; the hour was about seven,
He was talking about you, and how to get to heaven.

Now remember you didn't hear this from me, because gossip
I don't spread,
But you can all get to heaven if you practice and do what he
said.

His anniversary is coming up and it'll behoove you to say,
Tell all your friends to bring some money, because New
Destiny is where we'll stay.

He had a lot of bills as I was going through his mail,
All those responsibilities I just had to tell.

Now if you love Ethan Ogletree you should show some sign,
The LaStrappe's will, that's me and mine.

This is his eleventh anniversary, and you know were trying
to build,
If you are old and almost gone, put him in your will.

Pastor Ogletree's eleventh anniversary and we're all here on the scene,
Let's surprise him with a lot of money, if you're not too mean.

He takes a lot of time preparing the word of God,
Let's give him a lot of money, it's not that hard.

This is not gossip; if you pay your tithes don't raise your hand,
This money is for Ethan Ogletree, because he's a God sent man.

Remember, you didn't hear this from me, and now I'm through,
If you ask me who said it, I'll say it was you.

                              August "Bubber" LaStrappe

# CHAPTER 8

# LET THEM REST,
# IF YOU WILL

# JUST IMAGINE

*The Williams' Family*
*By Strap—April 2005*

Just imagine that we are all up in Glory,
Everybody here would have a total different story.

Just imagine we are all around God's throne,
Hearing God say how we all made it home.

Just imagine, just for a minute,
Your time on earth, and how you spent it.

We are so intelligent and we should never faint,
To know how God is pleased at the death of a saint.

Just imagine!!! And I'll use Rick as a guide,
Jean, he's not dead, he's just on the other side.

Ricky's time, it really wasn't that long,
I know he was saved, so God called him home.

Life is rough and we sometimes cry,
But, we will understand it better, by and by.

You can just imagine what our future holds,
If you trust in God, plus we'll never grow old.

Time will pass as we draw closer to our God,
But, the love for Ricky will never leave our heart.

I know it hurts, because I feel it too,
But if you give me a minute J.W., I'll tell you what to do.

Ye though I walk through the valley and I sometime don't
understand,
I know Jesus is right here with me holding my hand.

Job was a man, who though he was threw,
But, he trusted God, he knew what to do.

Just imagine in your mind that the yoke is easy and the
burdens are light,
Put your trust in God, and hold on with all your might.

God only call for the best, and that means He's real picky,
Well he sure got a jewel when he called my boy Ricky.
Just imagine when it's all said and done,
All of us together, praising God's Son.

# LEVYE DAVIS

Who was the man that came into my life,
Nothing but wisdom and a whole lot of advice.

Walking around his yard, me begging for some flowers,
He would be telling me about life; boy we spent hours.

Who was that man that I called Uncle Dave,
Like a father-son love that he so freely gave.

Whenever I was down and that seemed to be a lot,
I'd head out to Uncle Dave's and wisdom is what I got.

Who is that man that acted like my dad,
Levye Davis was the one, I wished I had.

He told me how faith in God would always see me through,
He'd say Bubber what I'm saying, that's really up to you.

Although my heart is sad and downright heavy,
I want the Jackie family to know; sho' going to miss my Uncle
Levye.

As I bring this little poem closely to an end,
When I get to heaven, oh I'll see my Uncle Dave again.

Levye Davis is with Jesus and Aunt Telitha too,
You know he won't leave that pretty girl just to come back
to you.

Uncle Dave is home now, up there with his wife,
If you want to see him again, that depends on how you
spend your life.

To the family, friends and love ones too,
I'm saying I love you, and now I'm through.

August (Bubber) LaStrappe

# (Mudear's Sister) From my Point of View

We can talk and then you can give me a queue,
But, what I'm going to say, it's my point of view.

Vivian Hamilton (Billy) didn't want anybody sad, and please
don't cry,
This is designed to make you smile, at least I'll try.

Billy was so pretty, and I'm not the only one to say,
She looked just like Loretta Young, back in the day.

Here we are sisters, brothers, and first cousins too,
There is so much love, cause that's what we do.

She lived a long life, but I'm selfish and I wanted more,
But, I do thank God for the time, at age 94.

This writing is to make you smile, and you might say it's silly,
Thank God for my auntie Vivian, who we all call Billy.

When Mudear left (Doris), I felt so all alone,
But, there was always Billy telling me to hold on.

I believe in the Bible and every day is a new,
Like I said in the beginning, this is my point of view.

I use to leave Seattle, and lay across her bed, and we would
reminisce,
I wasn't the only one, but that's really what I'll miss.

Pauline was the first girl from the sisters, and they bragged,
but didn't realize,
So I'd look up and say, Billy did you see my eyes?

I would talk to her every week, and this is the way it goes,
We both would wonder if a match box would hold our
clothes.

If I could sing a song, it wouldn't be sad,
I'd thank God for the memory, and relatives we had.


Jesus is tenderly calling, and we know not when,
So let's enjoy this celebration, and end it with a grin.

Good night Billy, and I will never say goodbye,
Oh when you see Mudear, tell her Bubber said hi.

As I close this note, Ruthie is giving me the queue,
I hope nobody is sad, but remember it's my point of view.

One last thing; I do remember Myrtle, Tommy, Mudear, and
Uncle D,
Billy just joined them, and now she's free.

So many love ones and friends have crossed over in my time
at age 72,
I'm trying to live right, and get to heaven; what about you?

This is the end of this little poem, and now I'm through,
Please don't forget what I said; that's my point of view.

P.S.
Brenda, Bubba, Drelda, Steve, Ann, and Paul,
This is big Bubber saying, I love you, now that's all!

August (Bubber) LaStrappe
09/21/2014

# Rooster "The Dude" Big Cuz James Hamilton

Johnnie Hamilton! I want to tell you something that's before your time,
Rooster and I met, it was around 1949.

As I remember it was Rooster, Hambone, and Red, I think I was around four,
The friendship we started, you couldn't ask for nothing more.

As teenagers, Rooster always stood tall;
Whenever we were together, I know we would have a ball.

He could dance real good, but he was not the best;
I won't call any names; I'll just let you guess.

Johnnie, when he met you I thought he had found the best;
Then I met Ruthie, again I'll let you guess.

In the middle 60's you were married and moved out of state,
A few years later I followed, that was March of '78.

I love you Big Cuz, and I will miss you too,
Trusting in God, He'll tell me what to do.

Johnnie, all things work together for the good,
Put your faith in Jesus, like you know you should.

I'll stop for a moment and we all will shed some tears,
But when Jesus returns, there will be no fears.

When Jesus returns and reaches out His hand,
That's when we can truly say, now I understand.

8/16/2008
August LaStrappe
(Bubber)

# SPECIAL DELIVERY

## *Mrs. Augustine Hollins*

Hi Nana Baby, surely you didn't expect this,
It's a letter from heaven and it's sealed with a kiss.

I had to get permission and God said the same,
You can only read this letter, its' signed in Jesus' name.

I know you are tired and you might feel alone,
You already know Jesus, so He'll welcome you home.

Nana Baby, you should see this place, the human mind don't
really have a clue,
The promises that God has made, and wow what a view.

Your yard is so pretty and I never will forget,
But here in heaven, comparison just can't be met.

When you get here you will be welcomed and no one will
be sad,
Then we both will be pulling for Jean, your daughter, and of
course my dad.

This place is for only those who trust Jesus, I'm His and He's
mine,
Read and study your bible, start at Romans 10:9.

As I remember, you only drive Cadillacs, supposedly top of
the line,
Just wait until you see Jesus, the one and only Savior and
the True Vine.

Nana Baby, if you are tired and need some rest,
Come on up to heaven, you've already passed the test.

I will close this poem by saying, Jesus is tenderly calling and
He's really, really picky,
I'm already in heaven; love, your grandson Ricky.

By August LaStrappe
(aka) Bubber Strap

# CHAPTER 9

# AGAPE' LOVE FOR FAMILY & FRIENDS

# CHARLES WESLEY BROWN
## *Guilty as Charged*

I remember your big smile, plus your angry expression,
The things I remember, left a lasting impression.

I don't know anything about these players, because I didn't play,
But if you allow me a second, here's what I have to say.

I was in the 8th grade when Mr. Brown arrived on the scene,
I saw this great big mans, and I thought (wow) this man is mean.

Watching you with respect and mostly fear,
My first thought was to run out of here.

Not knowing how to be a man or even having a clue,
You probably didn't know it, but I was watching you.

You beat me a couple of times, and I sure thought you were wrong,
Looking back now, that's what made me strong.

Coach Brown you are a big man, and I'm not referring to your size,
Watching you as a kid, kind of made me wise.

Seeing all these ex-players and I hope I'm not alone,
You shaped a lot of young minds, that's what mad us strong.

Charles Wesley Brown—thanks for your teaching and your
coaching too,
Bet you didn't realize we were watching you.

They should have called you when you committed this
crime,
I guess it's not too late, since this is 2009.

A great man, as I stand looking in your face,
They should find you guilty, and I rest my case.

August "Bubber" LaStrappe<br>2/12/2009

# DONALD RAY

I would like to make a wish on this property and this home,
Asking God to bless you and never leave you alone.

The family will be blessed at 1234 Mills Creek,
When you trust in God and His word you continue to seek.

A beautiful family I would have to admit,
Especially those twins, that's a perfect fit.

Donald invented a sprinkler system that's simple and plain,
Look on the internet you'll find it under Tizino's name.

He will drive anything, but he think the Beamer is the best,
Well I prefer a Lincoln it too will pass the test.

Come to our suburb you will see a yard that's really neat,
If you ask him about it, it can't be beat.

When he looks at his yard he expresses total joy,
I hate to disappoint you, I'm his lawn boy.

Sandra thinks Donald is the best handyman wherever he goes,
The truth is I taught him everything he knows.

Seriously, Donald can fix anything and does it on time,
He tried to write this down but it just wouldn't rhyme,

This is a cutie and it's just for fun,
Thank God for our friendship it's second to none.

August LaStrappe
12/11/2013

# MIRIAM

Somebody really loves you, I don't remember who,
I found this picture, and that should be a clue. Somebody
really loves you, and it might be scary, We love you so
much, and that includes Gary. Happy Birthday Angel, and
there's no jokes,
This is especially for you; that's Miriam Oakes.

**HAPPY BIRTHDAY!**
**HAPPY BIRTHDAY!**
**HAPPY BIRTHDAY!**

Ruthie and Bubber

# Miriam

It's a card that didn't come from the store,
Our love for you deserves much much more.

It's your special day so have some fun,
Tell Gary to kiss you or he'd better run.

Our love for you comes from above,
Just like Jesus peaceful as a dove.

It's your birthday and you thought we forgot.
Happy Birthday, we love you a lot!!

**Happy Birthday**
**Bubber and Ruthie LaStrappe**

**P.S.**
**How this all came about and how it was  made**
**I wrote it, Doris typed it, Lisa mailed it**
**and Ruthie prayed.**

# FOR MY SISTER

Just a little note and I'll put it in a rhyme,
It could have been better, but I ran out of time.

The world should know and I'm not ashamed,
It took them too long to put you in the hall of fame.

I knew you were great, way back when,
When we were just kids, I knew it then.

I am so proud of what you have done,
A lot of hard work and some of it fun.

My sister Pauline is the best in the whole bunch,
Everybody at Prairie View should take you out to lunch.

If Bill Clinton was a smart man, and really wise,
He would recommend you for the Nobel Peace Prize.

Pauline LaStrappe Barnes, you are the greatest in every way,
From your brother and that's all I've got to say.

Congratulations Pauline—your brother (Bubber) August
LaStrappe Jr.
Ruthie LaStrappe, his wife
Lisa
Doris
August III
Zachary Jr.
Demarquo


We Love You!!!

　　　　　　　　　　　　　　August (Bubber) LaStrappe

# I Remember

## *James Saddler*

After all this time, 30 years or more,
I remember James Saddler standing at the door.

The door of the church is Pilgram Rest,
He's telling everybody that Jesus is the best.

If there was an award for Christian of the year,
James Saddler's name would surely appear.

You might not remember me, but I remember it well,
The Deacon of the church had a great story to tell.

A former member of Pilgram Rest,
There was a family that stood the test.

James Saddler was at the head,
His wife and children did what he said.

A good Christian man in every way,
Just look at his life from day to day.

I grew up with your kids, you probably forgot,
Just watching the way you lived, I really learned a lot.

When God made man he had you in mind,
He knew you would be needed in this day and time.

Happy Birthday Deacon Saddler with all of God's speed,
Keep Christ in your life, that's all you'll ever need.

This poem is from Seattle, WA, and that's on the map,
I wrote if just for you, I'm August LaStrappe.

August LaStrappe
(Bubber)

**DEMARQUO LASTRAPPE
(I C)
RULES TO REMEMBER**

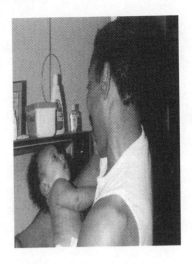

# INSPIRING WORDS FROM PAPA

1. READ OUR BIBLE AND KNOW FOR SURE,
   SATAN HAS TRAPS, AND HE WILL LURE.

2. YOUR EDUCATION IS SECOND TO NONE,
   STUDY REAL HARD, BUT STILL HAVE FUN.

3. LEAVING US, YOU'RE NOW ON YOUR OWN,
   MAKE GOOD DECISIONS, SINCE YOU THINK YOU'RE
   GROWN.

4. IF YOU EVER HAVE A PROBLEM THAT SEEM REAL HARD,
   STOP FOR A MOMENT AND JUST TALK TO GOD.

5. REMEMBER HOW YOU WERE RAISED, THE CHOICE IS
   UP TO YOU,

   LOVE FROM PAPA!! YOU KNOW WHAT TO DO!

# JUST A FRIEND

We checked the list looking for a friend,
The name that came up was Evelyn Enn.

We left Texas for this special day,
If you give me a second here's what I say.

It's your birthday, and it's time to cheer,
Ruthie and I left home just to be here.

To help you celebrate and say God Bless,
You are a true friend that pass the test.

What a friend is and you might not know,
One who brings joy to your heart wherever you go.

Just a friend we met a few years back,
Our love for you Evelyn, is still intact.

We left Texas and that's another state,
Only to say Happy Birthday, we think you're great.

This was to short for a letter, and to long for a card,
To love Evelyn Ennis, it's not that hard.

August (Bubber) and
Ruthie LaStrappe
05-07-2011

# Marget: Retired????

I'm here only for a reason, to see if it's true,
Marget sitting down with nothing to do.

Over 40 years you worked so hard, and always busy,
When I see you working, it kinda makes me dizzy.

You have been running and running all over the state,
Everybody knows that you might be late.

The way you work, always on the run,
The end results, you get the job done.

You work so hard running and doing the best you can,
You probably didn't know, I'm your biggest fan.

You are my BFF, and I call Bobbi too,
That's a threefold cord, that's really true.


I'm writing this poem just because I can,
You thought Bubber did it, but he didn't lend a hand.

Marget, born and raised in the great Northwest
Now you are retired, so give it a rest.

Congratulations on retiring, and a job well done,
Now come on to Texas and lets have some fun.

                                        Ruthie LaStrappe

# MISSION IMPOSSIBLE

Jessie Chatman; you, Tre' and Rob are BFFs. I watched you as a kid, a good kid, never in trouble and never went to jail. As a kid I watched you grow and that did pass: Mission completed. You went to college as a running back, you even broke some records and that too passed: Mission completed. You were drafted to the pros; San Diego, Miami, and the Jets. I kept up with you, and you did good, and that too passed: Mission completed.

Now you're retired from the pros and just got married: ***Mission Impossible!***

If you follow the world, it will never last,
If you trust in God, he will bring it to pass.

They say marriage is 50/50, and that's a lie,
To make your wife happy, you should be willing to die.

Marriage is a Mission Impossible, if you don't have God,
Keep trusting Him, you'll find it's not that hard.

To get a divorce is an easy scheme,
You married Davita, now follow your dream.

You didn't quit high school, you didn't quit college, and you didn't quit the pros,
You are married to Davita, now stay on your toes.

Mission Impossible and it can be done,
If you trust in God and His begotten Son.

You call me pops and I call you son,
Now catch my marriage, that's 41!

August (Bubber) LaStrappe
"Pop"

# NOBODY WHO TOLD SOMEBODY

My wife Ruthie LaStrappe, and best friend Marget Chapel,
Met Cora Lee Johnson with a story to tell.

Born down south and really poor and I mean po'
She couldn't thread a needle, but she wanted to sew.

Picking cotton at a really young age,
Hard work was challenging, that set the stage.

She did get married but her husband did her wrong,
Another setback in life, but that made her strong.

Her family married her off to a no good man,
She never had children, but that was God's plan.

She got a sewing machine and the books she read was only
three,
Her only goal was to help others and to set them free.

All her setbacks in life was only a test,
She trusted God, and He did the rest.

Clara Lee Johnson, a Strong Black Woman that you should
admire,
When you read her story that should start your fire.

The moral of this poem is to follow your dream,
Put God first, and join His team.

I did meet Mrs. Cora, and I heard her story,
Through all her trials and tribulations, she gives God the glory.

August (Bubber) LaStrappe
04-02-2011

# Pictures on the Wall

You should see the pictures that's on my wall,
It represents my family, but I didn't get them all.

Slavery is where my Lastrappe name began,
They mixed and crossed the blood, that Caucasian man.

Out of slavery the blood was mixed,
I lost my identity to somebody's tricks.

Five generations is as far as I can go,
They called us mulatto, that's all I know.

They crossed South Africa with West Africa and that's for sure,
But they were all black and the blood was pure.

They brought us over in the bottom of a boat,
You can't believe everything they said, or the things they wrote.

My great, great grandfather Etienne LaStrappe, the mulatto,
no picture shown,
We weren't considered human, just property somebody owned.

My great grandfather Augustine LaStrappe, the man stood tall,
He and Lucie had six children, and they are shown on my wall.

My life is an open book, and you can see it all,
The times of my father and mother by the pictures on the wall.

August (Bubber) LaStrappe
02/01/2010

# THE STEPFATHER

I don't like the word step,
The duties of a father he always kept.

I don't like the word friend,
He past that over and over again.

I don't like the word preacher,
He past that as well as being a teacher.

I could say my mother's mate,
When he married her, the whole family got straight.

The stepfather is big, the stepfather is strong,
In my eye sight, he can do no wrong.

Whenever I need him, he never left me down,
Just like a father, sometime I get a frown.

This stepfather is good, this stepfather is true,
Not many fathers are cut like you.

I love him because he's for real,
And he married my mother, that's part of the thrill.

Just thinking about the stepfather, and all his good,
There is no fault in his neck of the woods.

I don't like the word step, but it's a fact,
I only wish I could turn the times back.

Obie T. Dunson; the stepfather name,
Left up to me he would be in the hall of fame.

August (Bubber) LaStrappe
1975

# THAT'S A FAMILY

When he comes home and all is well,
The kids have been to school, with stories to tell.

They sit at the table, preparing for dinner,
Thanking God for His word, and praying for a sinner.

That's a family when love abide, and there is no hate,
The family comes first, others have to wait.

A family together when things are good,
If you ask for prayer, you know they would.

When things are bad and they feel ashame,
They pray to God, in Jesus' name.

If you're having problems and it creates fear,
Remember God's word, He's forever near.

God first, man second, the wife third,
That's family, not a discouraging word.

Solid as a rock, sweet and pure,
That's a family, and that's for sure.

August "Bubber" LaStrappe
10/1975

# WHAT I SEE

I don't know if it's true, but from what I see,
You have helped so many people including Rose Bee.

You came to Chicago with one little bag,
But, your love was big, you gave it to Mag.

You arrived in Chicago, right on time,
When Bernice heard it, she was right behind.

Four sisters in Chi Town and definitely on the scene,
You got together and said we must tell Betty Jean.

Like I said, I don't know if it's true, but from what I see,
The best one you helped was Ruthie Lee.

You helped all your sisters and you thought you were through,
You almost forgot the baby, and that's Mary Lou.

I know in the past you helped your brothers when they couldn't see,
That's O.C., James, oh yeah and Willie Dee.

I don't know if it's true, but, from what I found,
You are a loving, giving person, and that means you are heaven bound.

I don't know if it's true, but from what I can tell,
I love you Minnie, and you can go to....
The store and get the plumbing to fix the smoke detector.

Love Bubber
06/29/05

# When I be a Man

Lying on the ground wrestling, tussling or playing in the sand,
Little boys dreams of growing up and becoming a man.

Having fun with Bobby, my first cousin, and we did it a lot,
Cowboys, Indians and other games, some I forgot.

When I be a man, I'll be rich, buy a car, and be really great,
We both had the same dreams and plans around seven or eight.

I remember Bobby and I would fight and he'd always win,
He never tried to hurt men, I was his favorite kin.

We had so many dreams and expectation all in the plan,
The things we were going to do, when we be a man.

In our early 20's Bobby got married and I moved away,
I'll always remember the dreams of Bobby and I back in
the day.

When I be a man our biggest dreams was to buy mama a home,
We would have a big ranch next door and she'd never be alone.

Wrestling, tussling or playing in the sand,
Bobby and Bubber's dreams; when I be a man.

August (Bubber) LaStrappe
02/19/2010

# WITH THIS RING

*dedicated to my son and his wife*

With this ring that shine so bright,
A token of my love, both day and night.

Here's your ring and it does have a glow,
It means I love you, and the world should know.

You march down the aisle and my heart does sing,
Pledging you my love with this ring.

God is joining us hand in hand,
We will trust in Him to do the best we can.

Our love will grow with communication and trust,
Relying on God's word and that's a must.

As we join hands and two become one,
We will be blessed by God and His only Son.

I can go through life having very little fear,
You by my side and God's word is near.

My love for Jamila is strong as can be,
Bigger than the ocean or a raging sea.

As long as birds are in the air and fish in the deep,
The vows I'm making, I'll forever keep.

The seasons will pass from summer to spring,
A token of my love, is given with this ring.

August (Bubber) LaStrappe
01/10/2010

Printed in the United States
By Bookmasters